GW00730364

Above: *a range of 'seductive' products that can be so tempting but need to be used with discretion and sensitivity*

the visitors were enticed into handling the textile exhibit and rearrange its shape.

The quality of surface plays a strong part in the allure of fabrics such as silk and velvet. However, synthetic versions of these traditional fabrics may be used effectively to produce a range of compelling surfaces. Here we will not only extend the techniques touched on in other books but also introduce new ways of working with such materials.

Fabric manipulation, hand and machine stitching, bonding, beading, gilding and embellishing are all covered but the title gives us the opportunity to produce even richer surfaces and work in more complex layers and depths.

Inspiration for seductive surfaces can be drawn from numerous sources such as medieval architecture, distressed and peeling surfaces, natural forms, crystalline structures, luxuriant foliage, rust and decay and museum artefacts. A magnifying glass will frequently reveal astonishing richness in even the most unlikely looking objects.

Fashion will, by its nature, change constantly but its acceptance in mainstream art galleries over recent years has been evidenced in exciting exhibitions. Georgio

Armani, at the Royal Academy, gave an opportunity to see attractive and alluring pieces, many of which showed how elegant encrusted beading could be when carried out with a restrained colour palette.

The word seductive can imply decorative qualities and in the present textile climate there is less work that could be described in this way.

Artists such as Klimt and Gaudi have enjoyed a huge revival in interest and both display a passion for seductive imagery. The recent inspiring exhibition 'Matisse, His Art and His Textiles', also at the Royal Academy, celebrated the influence of decorative textiles in his painting.

It was noted in the catalogue accompanying the exhibition, that critics of this period of his work described it as 'shallow and self indulgent'. However he was reported to have said 'It's a bad mistake to give a pejorative sense to the word decorative'.

With such a vast array of fabrics, materials and techniques at our disposal we will explore the nature of seductive surfaces and attack them with focus and commitment. We hope that you will be encouraged to explore and develop them within the context of your own style.

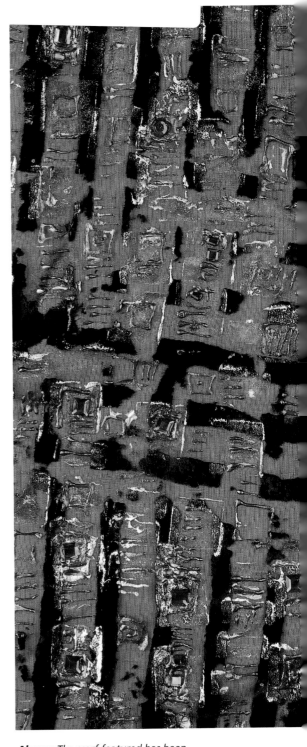

Above: *The scarf featured has been worked on a silk viscose velvet that was first 'etched' with devoré paste and dyed with black machine wash dyes (see Book 2 - Voluptuous Velvet).*

Further decorative elements have been added and they include. dimensional paint, gilding on trailed 'plexiiglue' and self-adhesive crystals. As a decorative piece this would be fine for special occasions but not withstand machine washing.

should be a fairly open weave that is easy to stitch into and for the heavier yarns a good large needle, such as a chenille 14, will work well.

Buttonhole is a traditional stitch with a wide range of practical and domestic uses. Numerous variations include *tailors' buttonhole, knotted buttonhole, detached buttonhole bars, buttonhole picots* etc. There are some magnificent examples of buttonhole stitching on fishing nets, lobster pots, Bedouin tents and many decorative ethnic textiles.

In the 1960's and 1970's buttonhole rings were widely used but are rarely seen now. They can be worked over curtain rings or other circular shapes but are equally successful when worked over threads. The simplest method is to wrap threads not too tightly around one or more fingers and then stitch a close buttonhole over the threads. They can be made fat or thin and this will depend on the number of times the thread has been wrapped around the finger or the number of fingers used.

Buttonhole rings may be distorted into organic shapes and will need to be clustered or integrated into a sympathetic background if they are not to look clumsy.

Building with Buttonhole

In previous books we have championed the cause of exploiting one stitch and extending its use by developing stitch samples.

It is worth repeating that the use of a limited colour range of threads helps to keep the focus on the structure and texture of the stitches. The threads can include a wide range of qualities and vary from thick to thin. Wires, plastic string, raffia and knitting yarns as well as traditional embroidery threads are all useful.

In order to make the most of limited stitching time it can be helpful to assemble a range of colour linked threads and place them in basket that can be kept to hand. The background fabric

The inspiration for samples seen on this page was organic surfaces. Plant forms, seed heads and exotic markings have provided marvellous examples of texture and surface. In a book entitled 'Heaven and Earth' (see book list) there are incredible images of natural forms and phenomena that are so outrageous that they could easily be works of science fiction.

Stitch samples are a marvellous opportunity to exploit surfaces and work in innovative ways. Experimental samples indicate possibilities that may be further exploited in more resolved ideas.

Sketchbooks or visual diaries are an important source of information for interpretive samples. During a beach walk on Raft Island near Seattle, there were the most wonderful barnacle encrusted oyster shells. They were the ideal reference for exploiting buttonhole rings and other textural stitches.

The initial location sketches were followed by larger designs. Watching the water ebb and flow over rocks inspired the encrusted beaded sample (see page 4).

Left: Illustrated here is the small sketch book carried on walks for instant sketches and impressions. The larger design was developed later using 'Koh-I-Noor' paints and fine line pen on rag paper. The linear detailing was worked by dipping a bamboo pen into black ink resulting in more organic and casual marks. An old encrusted shell was collected as a reminder of the walk and a good reference for later studies.

The contrasting samples both feature buttonhole rings. In the more lacey fragment they were applied to an 'Aquabond' stabilised grid which was later machined and dissolved (see Book 17 - Grids to Stitch).

The darker piece features the buttonhole rings applied to a gilded and embellished surface (see Book 17 - Grids to Stitch).

Below: The samples shown display some of the varying aspects of buttonhole stitches. They include buttonhole rings both informally constructed and worked over plastic curtain rings.

Buttonhole bars worked as raised loops offered the possibility of organic protrusions (bellow left).

In all cases buttonhole stitch was built up in layers and encrusted with beading or wire additions to construct dimensional surfaces.

Interpreting with Stitches

This embroidery (seen right) was inspired by lichen on paving stones observed after very heavy frost. The sparkling, encrusted 'collars' around each shape were very attractive. To celebrate this, the dimensional aspects have been exaggerated.

Eroded and painted foil was applied to a ground cloth and up to four or more layers of *knotted buttonhole stitch* were worked to capture the special qualities of the frosty crystals on the lichen. A range of knitting, tapes, wools, ribbons, metallic and iridescent threads were incorporated. Silver glitter paint and tiny protrusions of beads were added for further ornamentation and to integrate the whole piece.

To achieve the backing to the stitching, a foil packet used to store teabags was heated with an iron to distort it. Initially, the iron was hovered over the foil, which was protected by a layer of baking parchment. This action encourages the foil to bubble up towards the heat. At this stage, pressing the iron down firmly may create a lacy pattern! Time should be given for practicing so that many variations can be made. The heat of the iron and the pressure applied make subtle differences! It can be a little brittle but is quite easy to stitch into and can be most effective if used for decorative projects. However, it can be a method regarded as gimmicky if not used with discretion!

The foil can be coloured with fabric or acrylic paints (see page 16). As with all applications of colour to a cloth, care should be taken to burnish or merge the colour so that it is not too obvious. Slightly dampening the material first will help the colour merge within the background without any hard edges. This approach is appropriate for organic imagery but if a crisp pattern is envisaged another method of colouring would be selected.

Velvet Revisited

With a huge variety of materials and surface qualities from which to select we can really ensure that the choice of the appropriate fabric drives the ideas behind our work and is not merely an arbitrary background.

Velvet is a compelling fabric and its luxurious surface deters many from using it. However, it can be marvellous when a 'grand gesture' is required.

Such an opportunity arose with an exhibition inspired by the 5th Duke of Portland, an eccentric man, who lived in the middle of the 19th century. Having inherited Welbeck Hall, he proceeded to have rooms and tunnels built underground where he spent much of his time. His meals were sent down to him and the only daylight he saw was filtered through a skylight. He created magnificent gardens but his life was spent in shadows. The 'Twilight Pall' was a response to the challenge of celebrating the life of a man who seemed to exist in a strange underworld with the earth as his 'pall'. It required a fabric that could indicate shadows and mystery combined with formality, and black discharge velvet was ideal. Cotton velvets may be dyed with procion dyes before discharging (removing the colour) but for

this scale of work a black, commercially available, discharge velvet, worked well.

The leaves were printed with discharge paste into which colour was introduced thus taking out and putting in the colour in the same operation (see Book 2 - Voluptuous Velvet). Appliqué with machine and hand stitching combined to

produce an element of formality with an earthy half light feel. Dyed paper fibres were stitched to the surface to reinforce the feeling of the garden at night.

Above: 'Twilight Pall' (265 x130cm)

Top Left: Sketchbook study of decaying leaves using water soluble crayons, 'Koh-I-Noor' and pen onto a collaged ground, 'washed' with gesso.

In Contrast

If velvet on its own can be 'too rich a feast' it can also be combined with other fabrics to good effect.

Edwardian fashion often saw the weighting of delicate fabric with beads or velvet appliqué resulting in fabrics that hung beautifully. This combination of thick and thin, fragile against lustrous pile, can be extremely seductive. We can use such combinations effectively by mixing surprising surfaces, each offering contrast and exuding tactility. 'Petal Path', (see right) shows the contrast of cotton velvet on cotton scrim, thick on thin and matt against lustre.

The techniques involved are similar to those on the pall but the effect is quite different. Inspired by fallen petals on a spring pathway, the dappled light effect was achieved by sponging discharge paste onto a pre-dyed cotton scrim.

After ironing out the paste, velvet shapes were bonded onto the fabric but they were too stark and did not have the desired crushed muted effect. This was eventually achieved by using an 'embellisher' (see Book 17 - Grids to Stitch) and as often happens with experimental pieces, surprisingly, the reverse of the work was the most effective in interpreting the idea.

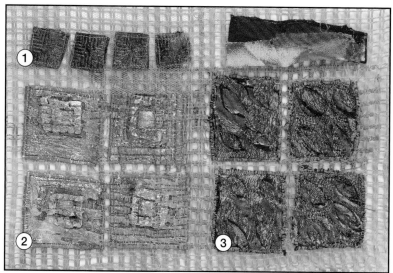

Through Thick and Thin

Continuing the theme of visual and textural contrast, the work on these pages explores other combinations.

Canvas can be another neglected fabric as it has a history that often implies order, repetition and rhythm in predictable combinations.

It has been used to glorious effect but rarely with other contrasting fabrics such as velvet.

Synthetic velvets have some properties that may be used to good advantage. one being that they can be coloured with transfer paints. This technique is still to be fully exploited (see Book 4 - Transfer to Transform) as it offers such exciting possibilities. Any light coloured synthetic velvet is suitable.

The triangular pattern (far right) was worked on a strong canvas ground coloured with acrylic paints. Transfer- painted synthetic velvet was then bonded onto the canvas. This offered the visual and tactile contrast that was further enhanced by hand and machine stitching. The nature of the canvas ground gives the stitching a different feel from that of a more conventional fabric.

A second piece (right) contrasts small scraps of devoré silk viscose velvet applied to dyed paper and worked on a canvas ground with hand and machine stitching. Some foil gilding completed the piece.

When people view textile samples it is fascinating to watch the ones that are most frequently picked up. Although colour is a compelling force in the attraction of textiles, surface contrasts, particularly those that include velvet are very seductive and often the first to be touched.

The piece entitled '...silk, satin, muslin, rags...' (see left) contrasts thin cotton velvet with silk. The silk was first coloured with silk paints before being overprinted with various fabric paints, stippled through stencils and printed with a variety of printing blocks including one for lettering.

Dimensional paint created the raised letters and foil added a touch of gold.

With so many different techniques used to create the printed silk scarf, a colour limitation was necessary to prevent an over fussy image.

The addition of applied velvet chevrons was designed to simplify the busy background.

This is a fertile area for experimentation and the canvas sampler (left) indicates possible combinations.

Sampler (left)

1: 'Angelina' fibres were compressed and placed on a wooden printing block before being ironed under silicone paper. The resulting embossed patterns were then stitched to synthetic net tulle.

2: layers of bonded and gilded synthetic velvets were applied to the canvas grid and secured with machine stitching.

3: layers of acrylic felt and synthetic sheers were first fused and etched with a heated stencil cutter and then stitched to the canvas.

The inspiration for all the pieces featured here are ancient books.

One of the points to consider when working in this way is that layer upon layer may be required to achieve the desired effect and it is often necessary to start with rich surfaces and then subdue them.

A typical example of this is the 'psalter fragment' (see right). This was a response to a newspaper article describing the finding of a medieval psalter in a peat bog. The book is over 1000 years old and is slowly revealing some of its former glory.

This piece has been worked on cotton rag paper and the techniques used include appliqué, dimensional paints, self-adhesive jewels, crystals applied with a specially designed glue gun, heat enamelling powders and stitch. Having produced a richly encrusted design the whole piece was 'bruised' with black puff paint that was then ironed with painted 'Bondaweb' and gently gilded with foil. The final operation was to iron on a black polyester 'chiffon' scarf and then distress it with a heat tool. The layering, heating and pressing hopefully mimics the natural distressing process.

Fading Splendour

There is something magnificent in the splendour of decay. Ornate surfaces in old churches and houses indicate the opulence of their former glory. Frescos, icons, baroque architecture and peeling surfaces offer wonderful inspiration for textile design and the opportunity for incorporating many of the techniques and available products in a considered context.

A visit to any museum, but particularly the Victoria and Albert with its miles of corridors, will give possibilities for a lifetime. The practice of keeping a small notebook and writing down references, jottings and notes is as always an invaluable way of recording ideas. A visual diary of a visit to Florence over ten years ago is still a valuable resource in the search for ideas and more frequently looked at than photographs (see page 12).

Distressed surfaces seem to have a general appeal and even the slightest hint of gold has a powerful attraction for many. How the layered surfaces in samples are achieved is a frequently asked question and the examples on these pages illustrate some solutions.

Top Left:
'Initium Evangelii III'

This fragment, inspired by ancient manuscripts, features a variety of fabrics applied to a stiff 'vilene' ground that had been prepared to look like old velum.

Machine embroidery was used to secure, enrich and enhance the image. Gay Eaton (1995)

Bottom Left: The contemporary book cover pictured has been inspired by old books. Onto a bonded and gilded background, adhesive copper squares, lurex fragments and machine stitching, have been further encrusted with hand embroidery and beads.

The small fragment (bottom right) also involves layers but this time the base is felt with layers of hand and machine stitching. The ridges have been achieved by couching down pipe cleaners for dimensional contrast. After working the textural image, the whole piece was covered with painted 'Bondaweb', foil gilding and a polyester scarf before being 'distressed' with a heat gun.

Polyester chiffon covered the prepared image to seal the surface and subdue some of the gold foiling before being stitched with both hand and machine.

Final detailing was achieved with a heated stencil cutter. Always wear a mask and work in a well ventilated space when using this technique.

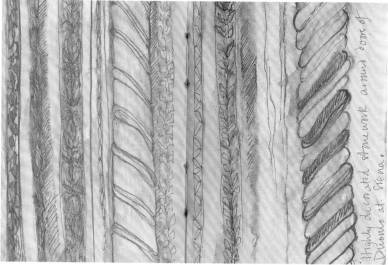

Medieval churches are an inspirational source of information for decaying splendour.

Photographs help but original notes and drawings contain more useful information. Location sketches are valuable and can be followed by more developed studies that may drive the ideas forward.

The design illustrated above is worked on card and involves layers of colour and trailing P.V.A. to form ridges in order to create surfaces. Textures have also been added with dark puff paint. This is a method usually used on fabric but it can be a good idea to explore some of these techniques at the design stage. Foil gilding was also used. Experimental notebooks can contain many of the 'so called' textile materials to good effect.

Viscose velvet has the advantage of a lustrous pile combined with the ability to be etched with a fine stencil cutting heat tool.

'Church Fragment' (far right) is based on a medieval alter frontal and describes the deteriorating surface of a once sumptuous and almost garish architectural piece. The fittings of such churches are infused with the history and have great appeal and inspiration for stitched textiles.

To create this fragment the basic shapes and structures were first bonded and applied using the same velvet as the background to give a more dimensional surface.

Heavily painted 'Bondaweb' was ironed over the whole image and then gilding foil added to highlight the detailing.

This combination of materials can describe old decaying surfaces very effectively.

Integrated Surfaces

When designing for embroidery, the first consideration should always be choosing the appropriate technique to help interpret the initial idea or concept. Thinking about the suitability of the fabric to be used is paramount.

Rough coarse materials and yarns may be the right choice for depicting old buildings and some rugged landscapes whereas the introduction of metallic and jewelled colours may well capture the essence of ancient icons or the interiors of some magnificent churches. Describing in words the surface of the design source can truly help the selection process.

Tree bark described as peeling, roughly furrowed, scaly, flaky, or like silvery, satiny, ribbons clearly indicates the first steps to take in choosing both the technique and the quality of fabric and thread.

Designs capturing the mood of fun, joy and exuberance will contrast greatly with subjects that may be more emotionally subdued. The choice of technique, colour, fabric and thread is always important.

However, in this book we are concentrating on surfaces that seduce and intrigue: ones where the colours 'sing' or the textures 'beg' to be touched.

Attractive, tempting, beguiling, bewitching, alluring, captivating, enticing, ravishing and irresistible are other words associated with the term seductive. These are all adjectives artists might use to describe their passionate responses to certain subjects, surfaces, colours and textures that excite them. In this book a broader interpretation has been used.

Textile artists can have excited reactions to certain colours, fabrics and threads. Observing embroiderers behaving at specialist shows is a delight to see. The allure of the feel of a particular fabric, the temptation of buying silks in exotic hues, the irresistible urge to buy more sparkling beads abounds. All at some time or another have bought some fabulous skein of thread that has so much presence it is always going to feature too prominently if great care is not taken.

In recent years people have been attracted to silk papers and captivated by a fabulous array of fabric paints, dimensional glues, multi-coloured wires and other mixed media that are now available to buy. So much on offer and so irresistible!

Above: *Based on decaying boats from the Aral Sea, this textured piece is worked on 'Lutradur' fabric that has been coloured, bonded, heat distressed and waxed to create an unique surface. Jackie Russell.*

Right: *'Field of Silver Diagonals' 5 Minutes from Home series- 46x59 cms. 2006*

A low sun, late one afternoon highlighted heads of barley presenting an intriguing glimpse of a rhythm of silver diagonals. Many of the thread and cloth fragments were placed on 'Aquabond' ('Avalon Fix') soluble fabric before machine and hand stitching to create a new cloth (see Book 17 - Grids to Stitch).

The secret for creating a richly decorative surface may be by planning the integration of stitched textural surfaces within the background at the outset.

Sometimes stitches, especially several different ones together, can appear as 'divas', each one trying to outdo the other. They display a big personality and can appear too important when placed on an unsympathetic background. In many cases the aim should be to form a pleasing and compatible partnership between the two.

For instance, a successful musical production should employ the lead performers, supporting cast, a chorus, costume and set design. If any one of these elements tries to outshine or perform beyond the writer or director's remit, the balance of the whole show can be ruined. The aim should be for the company to work together as a team. An embroidery can be viewed in the same way. The aims stay the same.

The term 'diva' can also be used appropriately when describing the overuse of some new products. Within a piece of work they should not outshine the overall design and some may need to be 'knocked back', integrated or blended within the piece. 'Tyvek', 'Angelina', puff and dimensional paints come to mind, although, if used with discretion they can add very attractive qualities.

The following suggestions may be helpful. These are not rules but they can be useful tips to ponder. There is never just one approach that will suit everyone. Obviously some artists have a different agenda and would approach work in their own unique way. However, the list may be beneficial and provide useful reminders to consider:

• The colours of the threads should tone with the ground fabric.

• Shaded threads can help to integrate if the hues are similar in tone. Very light and dark colours, mixed in the same thread, can prove difficult to control within a piece of work as they may well provide too much contrast and appear to 'jump' out from the piece.

• Painted 'Bondaweb' or fusible webbing can be ironed on the fabric for a subtle effect before adding fabric snippets and/or the stitching. Painted 'Tyvek' bonded down very firmly can provide an in-between link to help integrate the stitching. The embedded colour and sometimes eroded surface can be useful if treated carefully, otherwise it can tend to feature too strongly (see bottom left).

• Bonding snippets of fabric, thread, glitter, silk or wool tops onto a background cloth, which are then covered with sheer material such as a polyester 'chiffon' scarf can provide a link

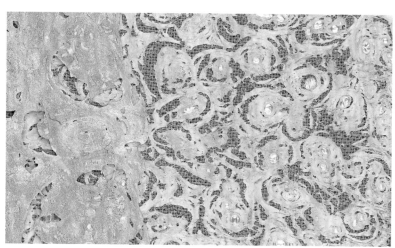

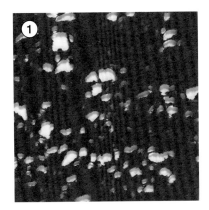

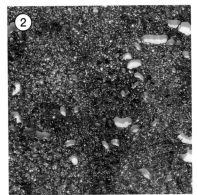

between the background and the stitching. This is enhanced if some tiny fragments of the thread to be stitched on top are placed with others on the ground cloth (see Book 3 - Bonding & Beyond).

• Scraps of scrim, gauze, fine nets and other pliable materials can be incorporated in the stitching process to create a more organic effect.

• Stitching medium sized and small stitches to blend in and around the featured area of stitches to give 'the mountains, lower ridges and foothills' approach as mentioned in 'A Guide to Creative Embroidery' also helps to form a partnership of textural stitches to the fabric.

• Gilding is another method of blending all the elements to rich effect. (see page13)

• Glitter glues and dimensional paint, if used with great care and sensitivity and applied to some of the stitches, can help link them to the ground cloth.

• Small beads used generously and stitched around and over the stitches and on to the base cloth, can also help integrate all the elements. To judge the effect, carefully sprinkle them randomly all over the work and with little gentle movements allow them to nestle in crevices etc. Take a digital image or make a sketch of the arrangement to remind you of the placements before removing them prior to the actual stitching in place. Remember to choose carefully the colour of the sewing down thread, as sometimes it should tone more with the ground cloth rather than the actual bead. This will result in a more organic look.

• Machine stitching, with toning, coloured threads, around and slightly encroaching the hand stitches can embed and unify them within the background in a more compatible manner. (see Book 9 - New Dimensions)

Above: *These samples illustrate the progress towards one method of integrating a stitched piece.*

1: 'Kunin' or synthetic felt eroded with a heat tool.

2: The felt painted with glitter glues. Remember to slightly dampen the felt to help the paint blend into the surface.

3: Sorbello and seeding stitches worked on the felt.

4: The completed sample showing how the glitter glues and beads have been carefully trailed on and over the stitches and on to the ground cloth to integrate all elements. Glues do slightly stiffen some fabrics and even more so if combined with eroded felt. The advantages include the ability to stitch without a frame and the surfaces created could be suitable for special cards, book covers, box tops and small bags.

Left: *An example of distorted tea bag foil. The method is explained on page 4.*

Far left: *This experimental sample inspired by ice patterns shows rag paper fragments, glitter and spangles bonded between sheer fabrics. Tiny crystal beads were sewn to integrate and add sparkle.*

Local fields observed over a period of time inspired both pieces. The first depicts the pebbly soil between rows of lush grass. Worked on soluble cloth, fragments of fabric and threads were applied. These contrasted with the many layers of haphazard cross stitches sewn with dyed silk paper string, linen and perlé yarns representing the grass. Tiny, shiny, glass beads were added to provide a contrast to the matt threads and suggest the glisten seen on the blades after a shower of rain.

'Ribbons of Mist' – 5 minutes from home series - 51cms x 84 cms.

This work reflects a continuing fascination of the effect of light on different surfaces. Due to weather conditions, time of day and seasonal variations, fleeting moments of changing colour and mood continually transforms the space. An early misty morning inspired this panel. Hand and machine stitching on soluble fabric formed a new cloth. An embellisher was used to integrate some areas.

Protrusions

Everyone reacts differently to a range of subjects and surfaces. Some people are captivated by the beauty of a sunset or are fascinated by the myriad of colours reflected in water. The velvety skin of ripe peaches or the rich glossy colours of cherries are all tempting to eat. Others find the allure of fresh falls of snow too much to resist.

Rock samples around the world continually attract artists. They are interested in their colours, textures, and geological or historic references. Walking along almost any beach, people will be seen searching for and selecting special stones, attracted by their colour, the glint or their smoothness.

Other qualities of surfaces that offer so much to appreciate are the endless ranges of mosses, lichens and tiny ferns that can adorn trees, rocks, roofs, pathways and statues in places around the globe. These protrusions are often fragile and delicate in their colouring and structure. Many prompt the reaction to caress and experience the feel of the exquisitely formed fronds or soft spongy mosses.

Plant forms, corals and seaweeds found on rock surfaces under the sea can be spectacular in

their formation and colour. Many display exquisite patterns and markings, while others move gracefully in the flow of the water.

Embroiderers have always been challenged to create works that exploit dimensional qualities. Padded surfaces can be observed in English Medieval church work, 17th century Stumpwork and some Victorian pieces. Wire, shells, bones, stones and more recently, bottle tops and ring pulls have been incorporated in a wide range of creations.

Many take the opportunity to experiment by layering stitches to build structures, exploiting the great range of effects that they can offer. The buttonhole stitched samples on pages 2-5 illustrate this point. There are many wires and other stiffening materials now available that can support fabrics and threads without them losing the quintessential quality of a stitched surface.

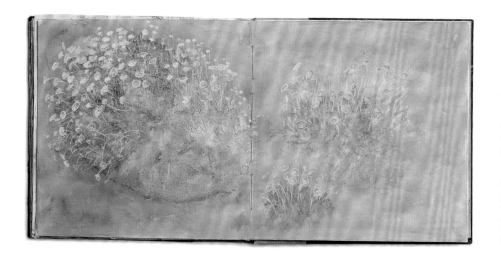

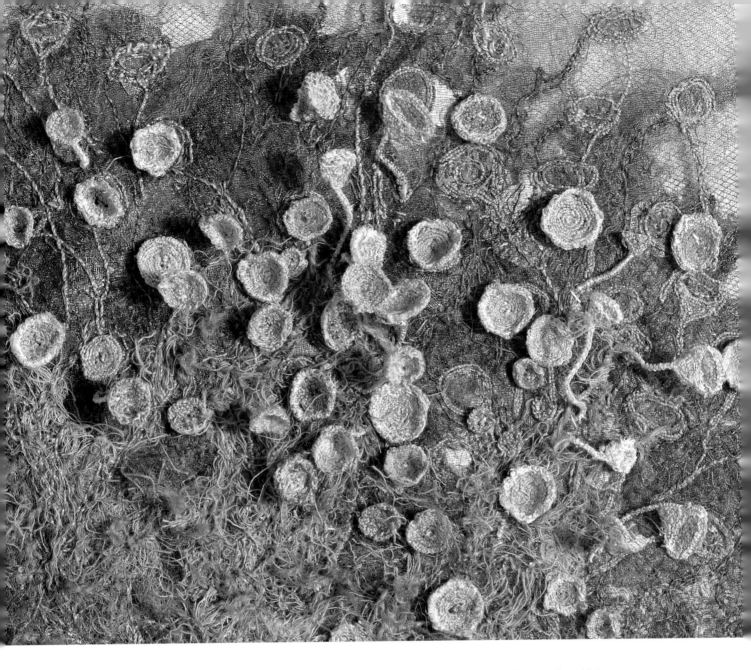

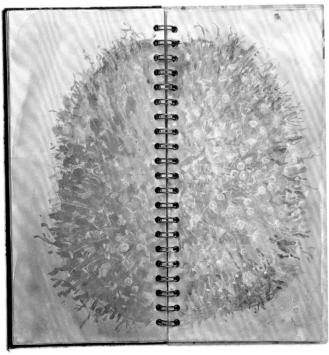

Sketchbooks: *Tiny fragile plants attached to stones under the water seen when snorkelling inspired other drawings. A stone was carefully lifted out from the seabed and placed in a bowl of sea water to enable a painting to be made. On completion, the plants were returned to the sea! Koh-I-Noor, gouache paints and pencils were used.*

Above: *This sample inspired by the plant drawings was created by applying snippets of scrims and sheers to a net stabilised by soluble film. Fine wires were covered with machined zig zag stitch. 'Solusheet' was used to support the wires as they were attached to the machine-stitched flower heads representing the fragile plant life. These were then dissolved and allowed to dry before being sewn in place and integrated within the main piece.*

Jewellery -
A Continuing Theme

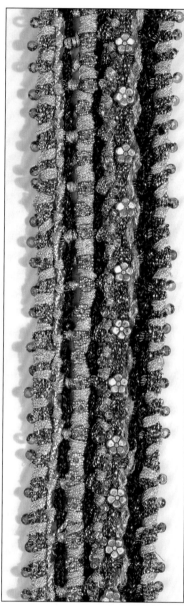

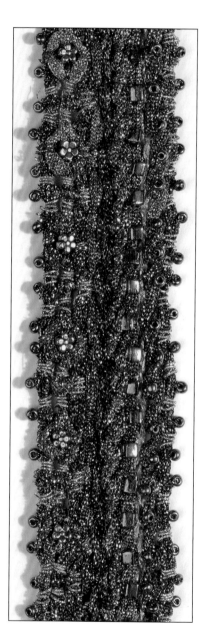

As stated in Book 17 - Grids to Stitch, attractive grid arrangements can be developed from a huge range of design sources. However, with a different focus or emphasis, the sparkle, gleam and decorative dimensional qualities of jewellery can be exaggerated to form opulent pieces.

In the first instance, a collection of shiny, metallic fabrics was made along with a vast array of metallised and twinkly threads, yarns, braids and tapes. These were bought from specialist shows and shops from many places. The availability of a fascinating assortment of beads enabled a huge 'stash' to be assembled.

The highly decorative cuffs shown were inspired by drawings of bangles and anklets. A variety of metallic braids and threads were darned or stitched over a network of threads set down on 'Aquabond' ('Avalon Fix'), a technique explained in Book 17- Grids to Stitch.

The original bracelets displayed a range of highly elaborate ridges and furrows and suggested the action of building up the surfaces by darning into the basic network of threads

then layering, wrapping and beading the yarns. The edges were over sewn and beaded for strength and decoration. A range of silver, gold, brass and glass beads were sewn on top of the stitching for rich textural effect.

Drawings of pendants inspired the delicate work on the opposite page. Again, metallic braids and tapes were arranged

on 'Aquabond', covered and trapped in place with soluble film. Because of the more complicated shapes and delicate arrangement, great care needed to be taken to machine the design in a toning coloured thread ensuring that all elements were very securely linked. For ease of working it is usually best to complete all beading before the ground material is washed away.

Conclusion

This book has offered us the opportunity to revisit some useful techniques and materials that have the flexibility and versatility to sustain continued experimentation and development.

It has also satisfied the need to explore some of the new materials on the market. We have only used those that offer real potential and it is good to extend our palette and not close our minds to new developments. Along the path some were found to be disappointing and less useful but satisfied the curiosity.

Experimental samples play a valuable role in exploring the vocabulary of textile practice but their true value is in the possibility for exploiting ideas.

A continuing thread in all our books is the marriage of techniques and materials in order to serve an idea. We hope that we have emphasised the importance of context when using products that can be viewed as gimmicks when used unsympathetically.

There are two main areas that we have to deal with when tackling work. One is the idea or impetus behind the work and the other is the technical knowledge that serves the idea. These can be simply described as the 'what' and the 'how'. Once we know what it is we want to achieve, the 'what', then we can use our knowledge of techniques, the 'how', to carry out the challenge.
We hope that the work illustrated in this book will help extend your technical expertise and encourage visual research into some of the rich fund of ideas used that inspire seductive surfaces for stitch.

Suggested Reading

Heaven and Earth (Unseen by the Naked Eye) - Phaidon
The Complex Cloth - Jane Dunnewold - Fiber Studio Press
Inspired to Stitch - Diana Springal - A&CBl
The Shining Cloth - Dress and Adornment that Glitters - Victoria Z. Rivers - Thames and Hudson
Matisse, His Art and His Textiles - The fabric of Dreams - Royal Academy of Arts.

Acknowledgements

Our greatest thanks as always must go to our supportive husbands, Philip and Steve, without whose help Double Trouble as a business could not function.
Grateful thanks also go to textile artists Louise Baldwin (UK) and Gay Eaton (New Zealand) and our talented students who allowed us to use their work, Michael Wicks our excellent photographer, and Jason Horsburgh for our book design.

Suppliers

A comprehensive list of our suppliers can now be found on our website by visiting www.doubletrouble-ent.com.

Double Trouble

Booklets in this series include: